BIG ISSUES

Brian Moses

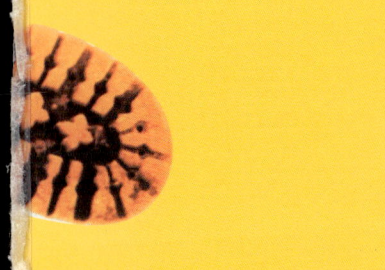

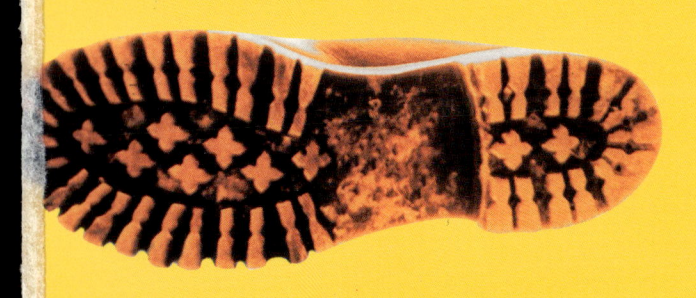

Heinemann Educational Publishers
Halley Court, Jordan Hill, Oxford OX2 8EJ
a division of Reed Educational & Professional Publishing Limited

Heinemann is a registered trademark of Reed Educational & Professional Publishing Limited

OXFORD   MELBOURNE   AUCKLAND
JOHANNESBURG   BLANTYRE   GABORONE
IBADAN   PORTSMOUTH (NH) USA   CHICAGO

© Brian Moses, 1999

The moral right of the proprietor has been asserted.

First published 1999

03 02 01 00 99
10 9 8 7 6 5 4 3 2

British Library Cataloguing in Publication Data
A catalogue record for this book is available from the British Library.

ISBN 0 435 09688 5   **Big Issues** single copy

ISBN 0 435 09687 7   **Big Issues** 6 copy pack

All rights reserved. No part of this publication may be reproduced or transmitted in any form, or by any means, electronic or mechanical, including photocopy, recording or any information storage and retrieval system without permission in writing from the publishers.

Initial design by Traffika Publishing Limited
Printed and bound in the UK

Photos
Stefan May / Tony Stone Images, cover (crowd scene). Sarah Lawless / Tony Stone Images, cover (boot soles). Martin Bond / Environmental Images, page 5. Collections / Paul Watts, page 9. Sustrans / Kai / Environmental Images, page 10. Collections / Ed Gabriel, page 11. Collections / Robert Weaver, page 12 top. Stephen Whitehorne / Environmental Images, page 12 bottom. Matt Sampson / Environmental Images, page 14. Gary R. Smith / Collections, page 15. John Morrison / Environmental Images, page 16. Collections / Image Ireland / Alain Le Garsmeur, page 17. Vanessa Miles / Environmental Images, page 18. Graham Burns / Environmental Images, page 20. Hubert Raguet / Eurelios / Science Photo Library, page 24. Gontier, Jerrican / Science Photo Library, page 27.

Illustrations
Illustrations by Vali Herzer and Traffika Publishing.

Contents

Introduction — 4

New roads
Does Havenhurst need a bypass? — 5
Arguments for the bypass — 6
Arguments against the bypass — 8
A balanced view — 10

The countryside
What sort of countryside do we want? — 11
Arguments for more leisure development — 12
Arguments against more leisure development — 14
A balanced view — 16

Fox-hunting
The sport of kings? — 17
Arguments for fox-hunting — 18
Arguments against fox-hunting — 20
A balanced view — 22

Vivisection
Is it right to experiment on animals? — 23
Arguments for vivisection — 24
Arguments against vivisection — 26
A balanced view — 28

Practical suggestions for expressing points of view — 29
Useful addresses — 31
Bibliography — 31
Index — 32

Introduction

In this book you will find arguments for and against four big issues: the building of new roads, the development of the countryside, fox-hunting and vivisection.

Not everyone agrees on these issues, and there are no neat answers.

After you have read about these issues, you may wish to discuss what you have read. Before beginning a discussion, consider these points:

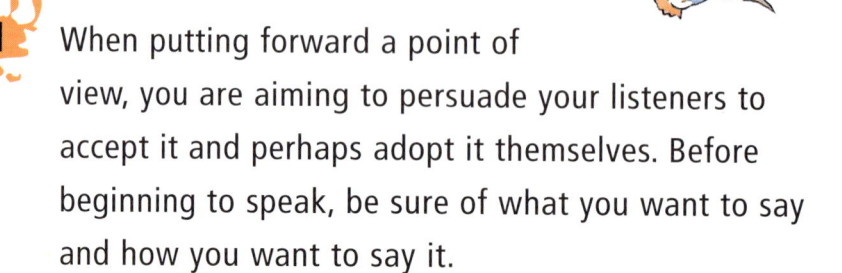

1 When putting forward a point of view, you are aiming to persuade your listeners to accept it and perhaps adopt it themselves. Before beginning to speak, be sure of what you want to say and how you want to say it.

2 Prepare for counter-arguments. Think about how your points of view may be argued against, and have answers ready.

3 If possible, support your case with statistics, photographs, quotes, etc.

4 Be prepared to listen to opposing views, and think about them carefully.

5 After the discussion, take time to think about how well you put across your point of view. Are there lessons to be learned for future discussions?

4

New roads

Does Havenhurst need a bypass?

Roads in Great Britain are very busy. Journeys often involve waiting in traffic queues, which can lead to drivers becoming stressed. Pollution from cars is also a problem that can affect health. But the forecast is that there will be a huge increase in cars, vans and lorries using our roads over the next twenty years. So how will we cope?

Everyone agrees that we need an efficient transport system to cope with our traffic problems, but people have different opinions about how this should be achieved.

Some people argue that more roads need to be built, particularly bypasses, which take the traffic away from built-up areas. Others feel that new roads simply create new traffic, as well as spoiling the countryside.

Let's look more closely at how this argument affects Havenhurst, a large seaside town. The main road through Havenhurst passes along the seafront and all through traffic has to travel along it. Over the past twenty years, the amount of traffic has doubled. Many of the vehicles are large lorries on their way to a ferry port.

It has been proposed that building a bypass around the town may be the way to solve Havenhurst's traffic problems. There are, however, arguments both for and against the bypass.

Arguments for the bypass

1. The existing road along the seafront was built for local traffic at a time when most people didn't own cars. It was not designed for the large amounts of traffic now passing through the town.

2. Motorists find it stressful to drive along the road, particularly at busy times when long queues can form. A bypass would help to cut down stress and reduce queuing.

3. The road is an accident black spot. Reducing the amount of traffic travelling along the road would make it safer.

4. Noise and pollution from traffic make life unpleasant and are known to be harmful to people's health. A bypass would improve the quality of life for people living along the busy road.

5. A bypass would mean that both local people and visitors would find it easier to get in and out of the town.

6. A bypass would create new road links to the town. This would attract new shops and factories, providing more employment for local people.

Traffic levels are set to increase dramatically over the next few years. Building new roads is one way to cope with the increasing traffic.

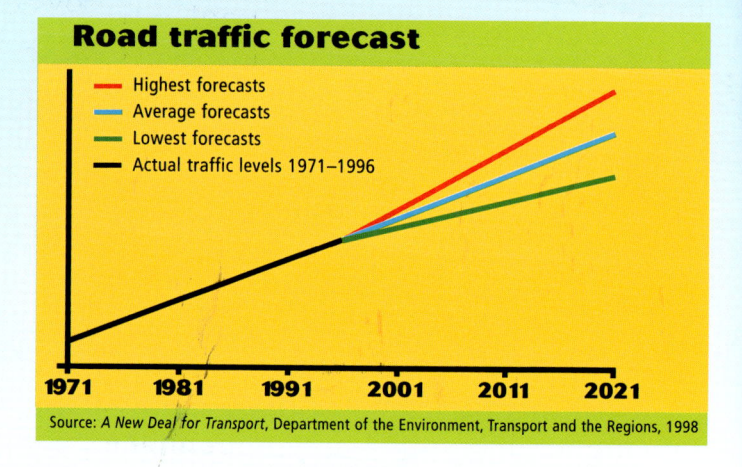

Road traffic forecast

- Highest forecasts
- Average forecasts
- Lowest forecasts
- Actual traffic levels 1971–1996

1971　1981　1991　2001　2011　2021

Source: *A New Deal for Transport*, Department of the Environment, Transport and the Regions, 1998

A letter published in the local newspaper, the Havenhurst Herald, from a supporter of the bypass.

Dear Sir

I cannot understand how anyone can be opposed to the building of a bypass around Havenhurst.

For years now Havenhurst has suffered from a vast increase in traffic along Havenhurst Road, and surely it is obvious to everyone that this cannot continue.

This road is a nightmare, particularly in the morning and evening rush hours, with cars queuing bumper to bumper for miles. This results in lost time and lost tempers. Also, the residents of Havenhurst Road have suffered health problems from both noise and pollution. If they want to move, they find it difficult to sell their homes because the queues of traffic and the general dirt and noise are off-putting to potential buyers.

To my mind, a bypass must be built, and built soon.

Mr R. Baker
29 King Street, Havenhurst

Drivers back campaigners

Bypass campaigners handing out leaflets to motorists caught in a traffic queue on Havenhurst Road

The controversy over the bypass makes a good story in the local newspaper.

Arguments against the bypass

1 Building new roads creates more space for traffic. A bypass would increase the amount of traffic in the whole area.

2 A bypass may appear to solve the town's traffic problems, but in fact the new road would just move the problems to another part of town.

3 A bypass would cut through areas essential for wildlife. The habitats of rare creatures, such as dormice, would be destroyed. As a result, many would die and the species could become endangered.

4 Surveys have shown that most of the traffic on Havenhurst Road is local traffic. This traffic would still use the existing road even if a bypass was built.

5 The money should be spent on improving public transport, rather than increasing the number of roads. Reliable and efficient public transport would encourage people to leave their cars at home. Dedicated bus and cycle lanes would relieve congestion and improve traffic flow.

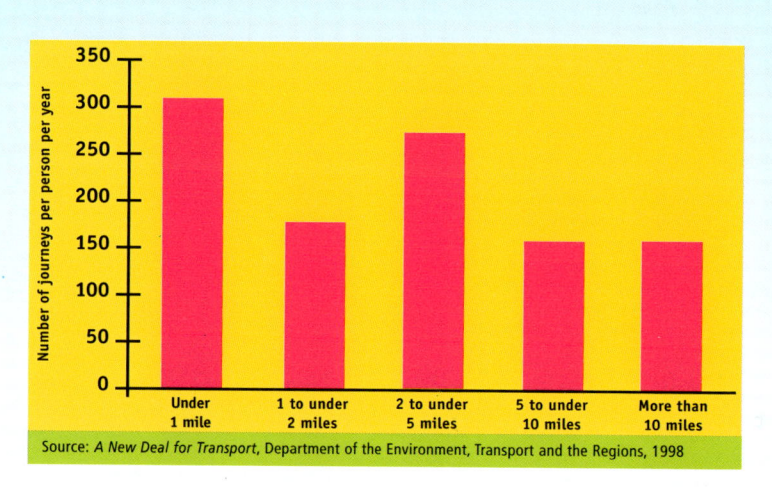

Source: *A New Deal for Transport*, Department of the Environment, Transport and the Regions, 1998

Most car journeys are less than one mile long. Traffic congestion should be solved by encouraging people to use alternative forms of transport, rather than by building more roads.

The local newspaper has also received letters from people opposed to the bypass.

Dear Sir

I refer to the letter from Mr R. Baker in last week's *Havenhurst Herald*.

Mr Baker feels that a bypass will result in less pollution for people who live on or near Havenhurst Road.

May I point out to Mr Baker that there are two solutions to this problem. One is that we should use our cars less, and the other is that the vehicles we use should be cleaner. I suggest that bypass supporters write to the government sugesting that car exhausts should be checked regularly to weed out the ones that give out too many fumes.

Mr Baker also writes that the bypass will mean less traffic noise. I should just like to say how much I love the countryside around Havenhurst where I often go to walk and escape from the traffic. If the Havenhurst bypass is built through these country areas, there will be nowhere to go for peace and quiet.

I say no to the bypass and yes to better public transport.

Mrs J. Giles
11 Roman Way, Havenhurst

A balanced view

Many of the people who live on the main road through Havenhurst are angry about the noise and traffic fumes. They believe that their health is suffering in the dirty atmosphere. Some elderly people claim that the noise gives them headaches and affects their hearing.

People also think that their houses are being damaged by the vibrations from heavy lorries. They are calling for a bypass to be built to take the traffic away from the seafront. It is also obvious, they say, that better roads can only result in growth, prosperity and a higher standard of living for all the people of Havenhurst.

Other people, however, are unhappy about the idea of a bypass. They say that increasing the number of roads very soon results in increased traffic volume, and that the existing road could be improved by providing bus lanes and cycle tracks. This might encourage people to leave their cars at home and make short journeys by bus or bike. They feel that the countryside will be spoilt if a new road is built, and that the traffic problem won't be solved, it will just be moved somewhere else.

The countryside

What sort of countryside do we want?

Demand for leisure facilities in the countryside is increasing all the time. On a warm Sunday in summer up to 18 million people take a trip into the countryside. Popular places attract thousands of visitors, so a great deal of wear and tear occurs in these places.

Over the past twenty years, huge changes have swept across the British countryside. Holiday villages, leisure centres, theme parks, heritage centres, open air museums, garden centres, water parks and visitor centres have all been developed to meet the needs of city dwellers escaping to the countryside for weekends or holidays. These developments have meant that roads have had to be built or widened and car parks created. As a result, the countryside has been altered as trees and hedgerows have been removed to make way for development.

New places to visit mean less damage to existing tourist sites. But is it time to call a halt to more leisure-related development in our countryside, or should we continue to welcome it?

The next few pages present arguments for and against the planned development of a holiday village, water park and countryside information centre in a place called Pine Tree Valley.

Hadrian's Wall in Northumberland has been damaged by thousands of visitors walking along it.

Arguments for more leisure development

1. Development doesn't have to be inappropriate to the landscape. A holiday village can be made of natural materials, e.g. pine lodges that will blend in with the local environment. A new reservoir can be used for water sports.

2. Many people like to visit the countryside, but not everyone wants to hike or ramble. People are demanding more facilities.

3. People who live in unattractive city or suburban streets have a right to escape to the countryside for enjoyment. Huge numbers of people visit leisure centres, theme parks and other attractions, so it is obvious that these places are wanted.

Windsurfing on a reservoir

4. Visitor centres can be used to teach people, especially children, about the countryside and how to protect it.

5. Development in the countryside creates employment in areas where many traditional farming jobs have disappeared.

Timber 'wigwams' in a holiday park blend in with the surrounding countryside

A letter to the local newspaper.

Dear Sir

I have read the letters in recent editions of your newspaper about the proposed development of Pine Tree Valley. It seems that some people are objecting to the idea of a holiday village, water park and information centre.

As the Development Manager of this scheme, I feel that I should point out to local residents how good this will be for them. The proposed lakes will be available for all kinds of activities including fishing, sailing, canoeing, water-skiing and sub-aqua diving. Around the lakes there will be facilities for pony-trekking and bird-watching. All the facilities will be available to local people as well as to visitors staying in the holiday village. In addition, it is hoped that the lakes will become the winter home of hundreds of waterfowl.

The countryside information centre will be available for local schools to visit whenever they wish. Along with an exhibition of life in the countryside, there will be a local studies room for schools to use as a classroom. In addition, this new development should result in over 500 new jobs being created.

Don't just take my word for it, come and talk to us at the planning meeting to be held in the village hall next Tuesday.

Martin Maloney
Country Park Developments Ltd.

Arguments against more leisure development

1 The appearance of the countryside is being spoilt. The countryside is often being developed with very little thought for the balance of nature.

2 Rising traffic levels around new countryside developments are changing the character of rural roads and making it more difficult to enjoy the peace and quiet of the countryside.

3 The countryside must be protected for its own sake. Hedgerows should not be uprooted to make way for car parks and picnic areas.

4 Insensitive development can mean that habitats are disturbed and, in some cases, destroyed. Wildlife that has existed undisturbed for centuries will lose food sources and shelter, and species may die out.

5 Too many visitors to the countryside can spoil its appearance through increased pollution.

A huge car park near a beauty spot in Dorset.

14

Dear Sir

I read with dismay the letter from Martin Maloney, Development Manager of Country Park Developments, concerning the proposed changes to Pine Tree Valley. I felt immediately that I needed to write to you to put the other side of the case.

The lakes that Mr Maloney says will offer us lots of different activities will only be made possible through the flooding of large areas of the valley itself. This is a valley through which I have rambled for much of my life. It contains a huge variety of plant and animal life, much of which will vanish if this proposal should go ahead. I am totally uninterested in water sports of any kind and would like the valley to remain as it has always been - a haven of beauty and quiet.

I have no time either for so-called information centres. Such centres seem to be popping up everywhere these days, even intruding onto the site of our local Civil War battlefield. I do not need an idiot's guide; my imagination serves me very well, and if I need to know more then I visit my local library.

This development must not go ahead.

Dr Richard Parker (Retired)

A monument marking the site of the battle of Flodden Field in Northumberland.

A balanced view

On one hand, there is a view that the countryside provides, and always should provide, an area of recreation for the increasing numbers of people who live in our towns and cities. People today have more leisure time, and the countryside is simply changing to meet their demands. Wilderness areas are still there for people to find if they wish, but there is now a wider variety of leisure activities available in the countryside as a whole. This is to be welcomed, as it gives visitors more choice as to where to go and how to spend their time.

On the other hand, if the countryside changes, it changes forever. Quiet places are far less easy to find. Many companies, keen to develop in rural areas, have no interest in anyone's desire to be alone when this is set against the chance to make money. Too much development, too many unpleasant buildings and roads clogged with traffic may well be the bleak prospect for our countryside.

Fox-hunting

The sport of kings?

The sport of kings – the hunting of wild animals with dogs – began a thousand years ago when the Normans hunted hares, red deer, wolves and wild boar, but it wasn't until two hundred years ago that fox-hunting became widespread.

Figures today show that there are over 180 registered foxhound packs in Britain, and that around 215,500 people hunt or follow hounds. Approximately 16,000 foxes are killed by packs of foxhounds each year.

The Countryside Alliance promotes fox-hunting as a way of curbing the fox population. It views the fox as a pest and a ruthless predator that kills hundreds of thousands of lambs, piglets, ducks, chickens and geese each year.

Anti-hunt campaigners claim that fox-hunting is cruel. They say that a hunted fox suffers great deal of stress and terror. The RSPCA* calls for a ban on all hunting with dogs, claiming general support among the population – a 1996 poll found that 73% of people questioned were in favour of a ban on fox-hunting.

Here are some arguments and opinions for and against fox-hunting to help you to make up your own mind.

* Royal Society for the Prevention of Cruelty to Animals

Arguments for fox-hunting

1 The fox is a persistent pest which needs controlling. 96% of sheep farmers believe that lambs are taken by foxes living on their farms. On average, foxes kill 2% of all lambs born, costing each farmer over £1000.

2 Hunting helps to preserve a balance in wildlife. It both controls and protects foxes. It is likely that the number of foxes would very quickly increase if hunting were banned.

3 Hunting is less cruel to foxes than shooting, trapping and snaring. All these can just wound the fox, resulting in days of suffering, followed by a painful death from gangrene. At the end of a hunt, however, the fox is killed instantly by a foxhound biting it on the back of the neck.

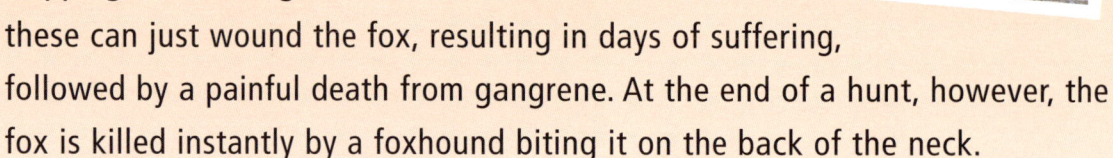

4 Hunting is important for conservation. Many hunts help to preserve the habitat of foxes and other wildlife. For example, they plant woodlands to provide hiding places, or coverts, for foxes, keep bridleways open and maintain hedges.

5 A ban on hunting would lead to approximately 16,000 people whose work is linked with hunting losing their jobs.

'It is a mystery to me how those who object to hunting fail to see the great contribution made by hunting to the British countryside.'

Robin Page, conservationist, Countryside Restoration Trust
(*Horse and Hound*, 22/4/97)

'The trouble is that people see pictures of cowering foxes, feel sympathy for the fox, and then immediately conclude that fox-hunting should be banned. There's no real thought about what effect such a ban would have on foxes. Of course, what would happen would be that far more would be shot, trapped and gassed.'

James Barrington, former leader of the League Against Cruel Sports
(*Sunday Telegraph*, 6/4/97)

'...while it is reasonable to assume that wild animals suffer from temporary fear and terror, there are no grounds for supposing that they suffer from apprehension to the same degree as human beings or that a frightening experience has the same serious or lasting effect upon them as it has on us.'

Scott Henderson Report on Cruelty to Wild Animals

'To farmers – particularly those in the uplands – the fox is a vicious killer ... control is an economic necessity for farmers.'

Farmers' Union of Wales
(*BBC Wildlife* Magazine, November 1995)

Some quotations from people and organisations in favour of fox-hunting

19

Arguments against fox-hunting

1 The fox is not a significant predator. Most foxes live on rodents, rabbits and carrion (dead meat). Foxes are scavengers – we see this in the town fox. Many lambs taken by foxes are either stillborn or ones that died soon after birth. Such lambs are weak and unlikely to survive anyway. Many more lambs die from cold, malnutrition or disease than are taken by foxes.

2 The fox population is not controlled by hunting. Studies show that where foxes are killed in large numbers, more cubs are born to maintain their population levels.

3 Studies of red deer have found that they suffer stress after long chases. This may well also apply to foxes. Evidence from vets has also shown that a fox doesn't die instantly from a bite to the back of the neck.

4 Too much is made of farmers' and landowners' motives for conservation. The RSPCA quotes a survey of timber growers who indicated that providing coverts for foxes was not a high priority when planning new woodland.

5 Figures for those who would lose their jobs if fox-hunting were banned are exaggerated. Less than 1000 jobs depend on hunting.

'The unspeakable in pursuit of the uneatable.'

Oscar Wilde, poet, dramatist and novelist

'The fact that lambs are found at foxes' earths is no evidence that they were, in fact, killed by a fox. The fox has the habit of collecting the carcasses of dead lambs and carrying them away for consumption at leisure.'

B. Vesey-Fitzgerald
(*Town Fox, Country Fox*, 1965)

'The scientific evidence shows that the fox cannot be classified as a pest and that, in any case, fox-hunting has an insignificant effect on fox numbers.'

Tony Soper, BBC Natural History Unit, Bristol, 5/3/86

'In my view there is nothing more disgusting than human beings killing animals for pleasure. It is degrading to human society and surely in particular degrades those involved. All those who believe in civilised behaviour should call for an end to blood sports.'

Eric Heffer MP (quoted in P. Windeatt, *The Hunt and the Anti-hunt*)

Some quotations from people and organisations opposed to fox-hunting

A balanced view

Those who support fox-hunting argue that it helps to keep down the number of foxes to a reasonable level. They say that lambs are killed by foxes and that these losses cost farmers, particularly small hill farmers, a lot of money. Hunt supporters claim that their sport is not cruel, and that when a fox is killed it is killed instantly. Foxhounds, they say, always kill swiftly to avoid being bitten themselves. The reason that many people are against hunting may well be simply that they don't understand what happens at a hunt.

Those who oppose hunting often do so because they feel that foxes are misunderstood creatures. They say that the fox plays an important role in the countryside by keeping down the rabbit population. Opponents of hunting also claim that fox-hunting is cruel, and that there are many occasions where foxes are not killed quickly. They feel that hunt supporters take pleasure in the distress and eventual death of a wild creature.

A leaflet from the League Against Cruel Sports, an organisation that campaigns against fox-hunting.

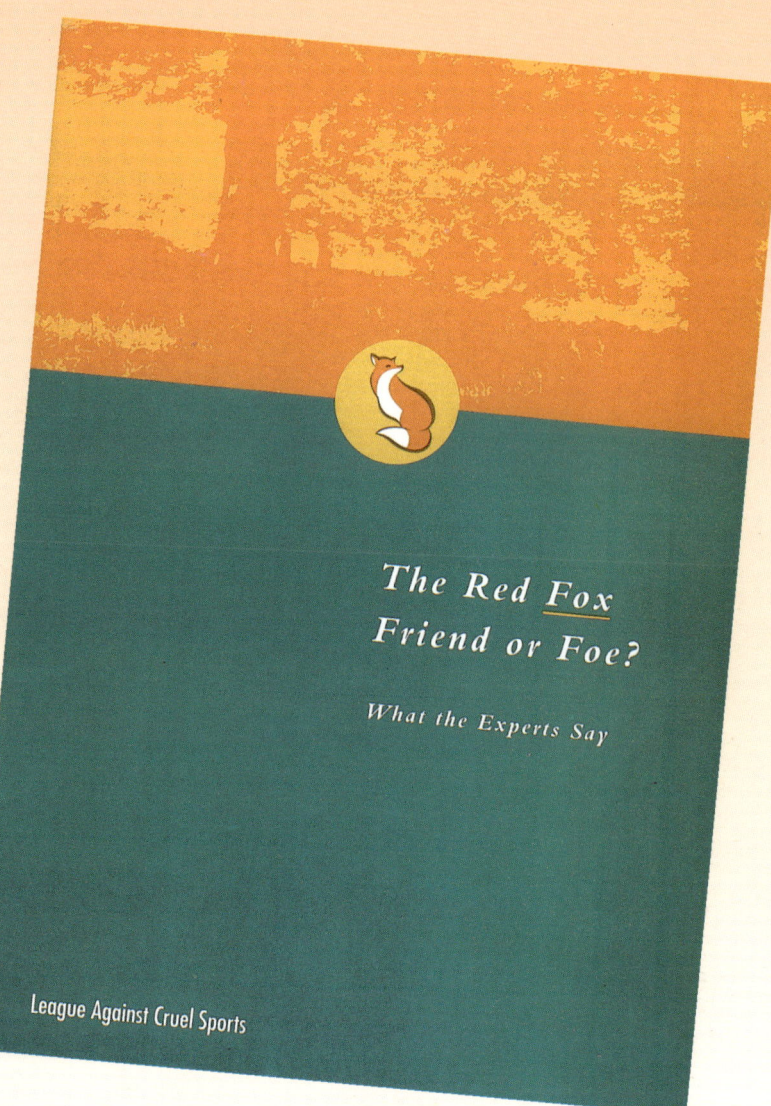

The Red Fox Friend or Foe?

What the Experts Say

League Against Cruel Sports

Vivisection

Is it right to experiment on animals?

Every year over 3.5 million animals are used in experiments in British laboratories. Many of these experiments are for the purposes of medical research, and many animals die in the search for new drugs to cure diseases.

Experimentation on living animals is called vivisection. Rats and mice are most commonly used in vivisection, although cats, dogs, rabbits, monkeys, birds, frogs and armadillos may also be used. Many experiments involve animals being used in operations or infected with dangerous diseases.

While most people now agree that testing cosmetics on animals is undesirable, opinion is still split as to whether animals should be used in medical research.

Many people would argue that animals' lives should be sacrificed so that human beings may be saved. They believe that humans are special and should take priority over other animals. Supporters of vivisection claim that it has resulted in enormous advances in health care for humans.

The opposite view is that all the Earth's creatures have equal rights, and we have no moral right to use animals for medical experiments solely for the benefit of humankind. Scientists have been experimenting on animals for decades, but still have not found cures for the major killers – cancer, heart disease and AIDS.

The following pages explore the arguments for and against experiments on animals. Can vivisection be justified?

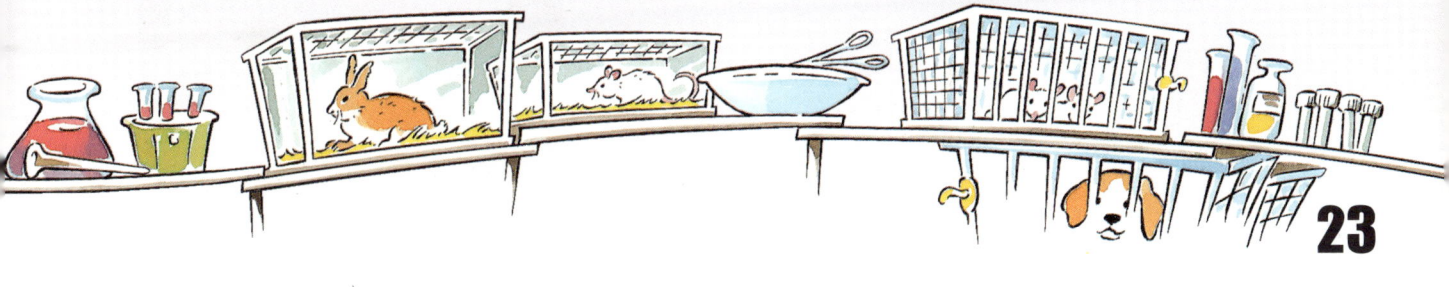

Arguments for vivisection

1 Experiments on animals are essential in the search for new drugs. Many fatal diseases of the past, such as smallpox, polio and tuberculosis, are now under control because of medicines and vaccines which were first tested on animals.

2 Animal experiments provide information on the effects of various medicines and treatments. By studying these effects, scientists can develop guidelines for the use of such treatments on people.

3 Surgeons learn how to carry out life-saving operations such as transplants and the removal of tumours through trying out such techniques on animals.

4 Although it is often believed otherwise, scientists do care about the animals that they use in laboratories. There are strict controls governing the day-to-day welfare of laboratory animals, and before a project is approved the benefits of the research to humans must be weighed against the possible distress that the animal may suffer.

5 Nowadays, computer and test-tube research play a vital part in giving scientists information. But it is only after medicines have been tested on animals that doctors have sufficient information to consider testing them on human patients.

This rat is being used in an experiment to investigate sleep patterns. It is hoped that this will lead to a cure for sleep disorders in humans.

Medical achievements

The following medical advances could not have been achieved without animal experimentation:

- Vaccines that protect against many illnesses such as polio, tuberculosis, measles, rubella, tetanus, hepatitis B, meningitis, distemper in dogs and enteritis in cats.

- Drugs and treatments that allow people with epilepsy, asthma and diabetes to lead a full and normal life.

- Cures for previously fatal diseases, such as Hodgkin's disease and childhood leukaemia.

- Modern anaesthetics and other medicines which make safe surgery possible.

Some of the major medical achievements of the twentieth century. Animal experimentation was used in the development of all these treatments.

Animal welfare

Scientists are concerned for the well-being of laboratory animals. The '3 Rs' are accepted as the basic principles of good practice in the care and welfare of laboratory animals:

- **R**eplace the use of animals wherever possible
- **R**efine tests to cause animals the least possible distress
- **R**educe the number of animals needed to a minimum

1920s	Insulin
1930s	Modern anaesthetics
1940s	Penicillin
1950s	Kidney transplants, polio vaccine, hip replacement
1960s	Corneal transplants, medicines for schizophrenia
1970s	Modern medicines for ulcers and asthma
1980s	Life support systems for premature babies, medicines to treat viral infections
1990s	Meningitis vaccine, gene therapy

Arguments against vivisection

1 Experiments on animals are not necessary in the search for new drugs. Many diseases were in decline by the time vaccines were developed because of better housing, food and drinking water.

2 Testing drugs on animals can produce unreliable results. Animal experiments tell us about animals, not humans.

3 Many diseases could be prevented if people were prepared to change their lifestyles by, for example, stopping smoking. This would result in fewer animal experiments to test the safety of drugs.

4 Despite the safeguards, laboratory animals still suffer a great deal of pain. Many experiments are carried out without the use of anaesthetics. In addition, animals are often kept in inappropriate conditions.

5 There are alternatives to animal experiments and scientists should be using these methods wherever possible.

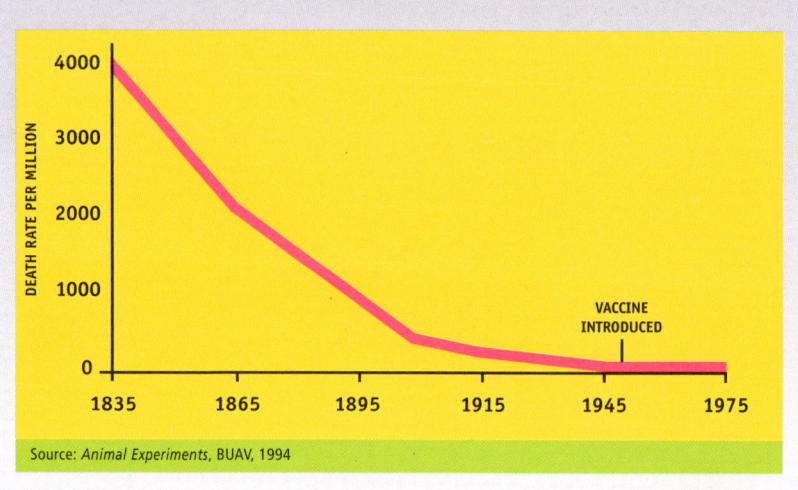

Source: *Animal Experiments*, BUAV, 1994

This graph shows the number of people who died from tuberculosis in England and Wales between 1835 and 1975. Improvements in health meant that the disease had almost disappeared even before a vaccine was introduced.

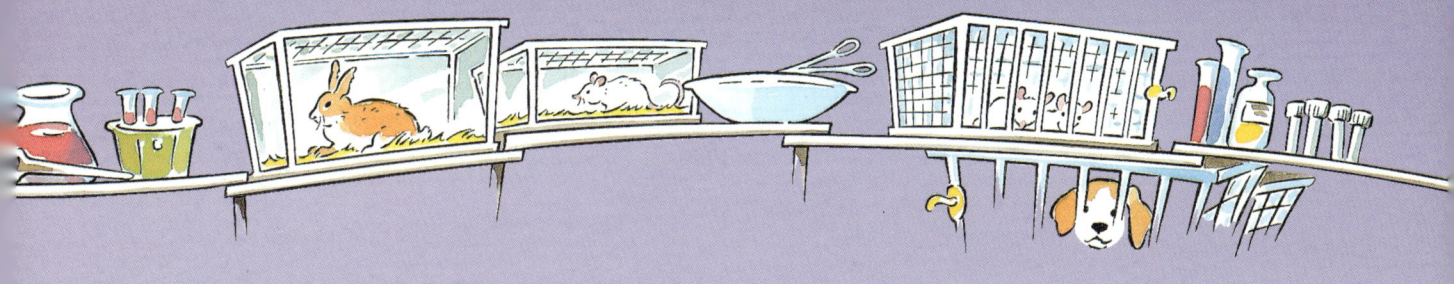

Unreliable results

Can we trust the evidence of experiments on animals?

- If penicillin had been tested on guinea pigs or hamsters, we would never have benefited from this useful drug – because it kills them.

- Morphine has a calming effect on people – but it makes cats frenzied.

- Aspirin causes birth deformities in many species including cats, dogs and rats – but not in humans.

- Thalidomide, a drug to prevent morning sickness in pregnancy, caused terrible deformities in humans – but not on the mice and rats it was tested on before it was marketed.

- The heart drug Eraldin caused serious side-effects including blindness in people – but it had caused no problems in animal experiments.

- Opren cured arthritis in laboratory rats – but when it was given to humans, there were 3500 reports of side-effects and more than 60 deaths in Britain alone.

(from *Animal Kind, Early Times*, 1991)

Monkeys often suffer a great deal when they are used in experiments. They are social creatures used to living in large groups. They become nervous and stressed when kept in laboratories.

27

A balanced view

Research on animals has made possible many different operations on humans. These include kidney and heart transplants. Experiments with rats, mice and baboons led to a treatment for epilepsy. This now allows most epilepsy sufferers to lead almost normal lives. For these reasons, many people believe that if human suffering and death can be prevented through knowledge gained from vivisection, then this practice is entirely justified.

On the other hand, it has been proved that relying on animal tests can be dangerous. Drugs have been released for human use and then found to be unsafe, causing further illness and even death. Thousands of animals suffer each day in tests that may in the end prove to have little value.

A leaflet produced by the British Union for the Abolition of Vivisection (BUAV).

Practical suggestions for expressing points of view

Now that you've seen some different ways of expressing points of view on these important issues, you may wish to make your views known to a wider audience. Make sure that you are as fully informed as possible about the issue that concerns you. You can do this by writing to request information from one of the organisations that reflects your views. Some of these are listed on page 31 of this book. Unless you know the name of the person you are writing to, address the letter to the Publicity Officer and begin it 'Dear Sir/Madam'.

You may wish to write to a young people's magazine, outlining your views on fox-hunting or vivisection. If there is a traffic problem in your area, you could try writing to the local paper. In both instances, address your letter to the Editor.

Canvass opinions around your school. How many others support your views? What would they like to see done in the future?

You may wish to publicise the issue that concerns you. Perhaps you will be allowed to use a notice board for pinning up posters that you have designed. Make sure that the posters are eye-catching so that people will want to stop and read them.

29

Try to compose a suitable slogan for the issue. It should be something that is easily remembered. Alliteration, repetition or a play on words can sometimes help. Look in newspapers to find how journalists make use of this technique.

Ask if you can talk about the issue in a school assembly where articles may be read out, poems and plays performed and posters displayed. You could consider presenting an assembly as a radio or TV broadcast with different people being interviewed about their views.

Contact your local radio station to see if they have any time when you could express your views on air in their studio.

As your campaign grows, you will probably think of further ways in which to get your message to a wider audience.

Good luck!

Useful addresses

New roads
Department of Transport, 2 Marsham Street, London, SW1 P 3EB
Transport 2000, Walkden House, 10 Melton Street, London, NW1 2EJ

The countryside
Council for the Protection of Rural England, 25 Buckingham Palace Road, London, SW1W 0PP
Campaign for the Countryside (same address as above)

Fox-hunting
Countryside Alliance, The Old Town Hall, 367 Kennington Road, London, SE11 4PT
League Against Cruel Sports, 83–87 Union Street, London, SE1 1SG
RSPCA, Causeway, Horsham, West Sussex, RH12 1HG
The International Fund for Animal Welfare, Warren Court, Park Road, Crowborough, East Sussex, TN6 2GA

Vivisection
Seriously Ill for Medical Research, P.O. Box 504, Dunstable, Bedfordshire, LU6 2LU
Animals in Medicines Research Information Centre, 12 Whitehall, London, SW1A 2DY
British Union for the Abolition of Vivisection, 16a Crane Grove, London, N7 8LB
National Anti-Vivisection Society, 261 Goldhawk Road, London, W12 9PE

Bibliography

Barton, Miles, *Animal Rights* (Franklin Watts, 1989)

Bright, M., *Traffic Pollution* (Franklin Watts, 1991)

Bronze, Lewis; Heathcote, Nick; and Brown, Peter, *The Blue Peter Green Book* (BBC Books / Sainsbury's, 1990)

James, Barbara, *Animal Rights* (Wayland, 1990)

Moses, Brian, *Somewhere to Be – Language and the Environment* (A resource book for teachers at KS2) (WWF, 1992)

The organisations in the 'Useful addresses' section above also produce useful leaflets and other publications about the issues discussed in this book.

Index

AIDS 23
anaesthetics 25, 26
buses 8, 10
bypasses 5–10
cancer 23
car parks 11, 14
cars 5–10
conservation 18–20
cosmetics 23
countryside 4, 5, 9–14, 16, 19, 22
cycles 8, 10
diseases 23–26
drugs 23–28
experiments 23–28
farmers 18–20, 22
foxes 17–21
foxhounds 17, 18, 22
fox-hunting 4, 17–22, 29, 31
Havenhurst 5–7, 9, 10
health 5–7, 10, 23, 26
heart disease 23
holiday villages 10–13
jobs 12, 13, 18, 20
lambs 17, 18, 20–22
leisure 11, 12, 14, 16

lorries 5, 10
medical research 23
medicine 24, 25
nature 14
noise 6, 7, 10
Pine Tree Valley 11, 13, 15
polio 24, 25
pollution 5–7, 9, 14
reservoirs 12
roads 4–8, 10, 11, 14, 16, 31
smallpox 24, 26
traffic 5–10, 14, 16, 29
transport 5
tuberculosis 24–26
vaccines 24–26
vivisection 4, 23, 24, 26, 28, 29, 31
wildlife 8, 14, 18

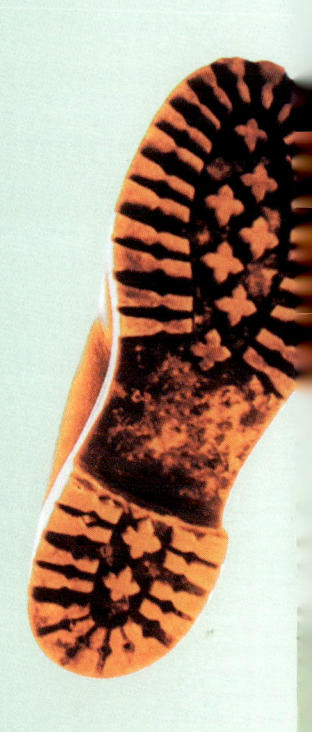